Scale To NEW HEIGHTS!

The Drury Gazette Staff
Gary Drury, Author / Editor / Journalist / Minister / Publisher

© 2016 by Gary Drury / The Drury Gazette

All rights reserved. No part of this publication may be reproduced or transmitted in whole or in part in any form or by any means, electronic or mechanical, including photocopy, recording, or any information storage and retrieval system, known or unknown, without permission in writing from the publisher, except by a reviewer who may quote brief passages in a review to be printed in a newspaper, magazine or journal.

I reserve the exclusive right to edit, accept or reject any submission for any reason whatsoever without verbal or written notice. The author bears sole responsibility for his/her own work. The expression within this publication reflects the beliefs and philosophies of their originators and are not the views and opinions of Gary Drury Publishing Ministries or The Drury Gazette.

Contact Information: No Phone Calls Accepted without prior appointment. For expedited correspondence please visit www.druryspublishing.com.

Serious inquiries ONLY, please. Spammers will be reported to their ISPs, authorities and legal action may ensue.

The Drury Gazette promotes raising authors. Its a non-profit private corporation sole ministry encourages strong Christian values, defends and supports inalienable rights, The Republic-United States of America Constitution: freedoms of press, religion & speech, etc. *26 U.S. Code § 508 (c) (1) (A). Gifts are tax deductible.

The Drury Gazette Digital is provided free of charge. Please adhere to any ©, ™, and SM mark laws. Nonetheless, this PDF must remain whole perpetually. No alterations permitted. Also, we encouraged you to share, however, not to sell, lease, rent or monetize the PDFs in any way whatsoever.

Permission is granted you to print out a copy for your own personal use. Absolutely, no authorization deduced for mass printed dissemination. The authorization is granted for email broadcasting provided no spamming and you are authorized to email such parties. Likewise, share with others to help spread God's word and authors gain recognition.

You can direct individuals interested in The Drury Gazette to www.druryspublishing.com to download a FREE issue. Enjoy!

SPRING 2016

Issue 2 Volume 10

ISBN-13: 978-0692699843
(Gary Drury Publishing)

ISSN: 1930-0875 (Print)
ISSN: 1930-0883 (PDF)

Gary Drury, Editor/Publisher. Established in 1982, Promotes well-grounded moral and spiritual values of all beliefs and faiths. I am devoted to creative expression and free speech. Correspondence, submissions, supportive donations and subscriptions should be directed to the publisher.

The Drury Gazette © ™ by Gary Drury Ministries © ™
www.druryspublishing.com © ™

NON-PROFIT QUARTERLY PUBLICATION
508 (c) (1) (A)

Cover photo, design, and layout by Gary Drury © ™

Printed in The Republic-United States of America.

Contents

PET HEAVEN	7
— © C. David Hay	7
SILENT TWILIGHT	7
— © C. David Hay	7
A GRAIN OF SAND	7
— © Betty Lou Hebert	7
RED SUNSET	7
— © Betty Lou Hebert	7
A PRECIOUS DAY	8
— © Betty Lou Hebert	8
TRUE LOVE	8
— © Herbert Jerry Baker	8
WHAT IS IT?	8
— © Ken Gillespie	8
SOFT WHISPERS II	9
— © Ken Gillespie	9
DAVE'S READY	9
— © Sheryl L. Nelms	9
LOVERS WALK THE BEACH	11
— © Sheila B. Roark	11
KEEPER OF THE PAST	11
— © Betty Lou Hebert	11
TOGETHER AGAIN	16
— © Sheila B. Roark	16
A MAN FROM DAKOTA	16
— © Betty Lou Hebert	16
FRESH MEMORIES	17
— © Betty Lou Hebert	17
I SAW MY NAME IN THE SKY	17
— © Gerald Heyder	17
SEDGWICK COUNTY JUVENILE OFFICER	18
— © Sheryl L. Nelms	18
LIGHT	18
— © Gary Drury	18
SECRET PLACE	19
— © Sheila B. Roark	19
HERE COMES THE SNOW	19
— © Sheila B. Roark	19
ANOTHER YEAR	19
— © Sheila B. Roark	19
THE ELOQUENT EYES	19
— © Adolf P. Shvedchikov	19
MY FANTASIES ARE ENDLESS, YES!	20
— © Adolf P. Shvedchikov	20
THE WORLD WILL BE SAVED BY BEAUTY AND ART	20
— © Adolf P. Shvedchikov	20
THE WIND DOESN'T BLOW	20
— © Adolf P. Shvedchikov	20
KANSAS COMFORT	20
— © Sheryl L. Nelms	20
IN GRAM'S GARDEN	21
— © Sheryl L. Nelms	21
GALVESTON'S EBB AND FLOW	21
— © Sheryl L. Nelms	21
BLACK HILLS SPRING	21
— © Sheryl L. Nelms	21
BUTTERFLY IN FLIGHT	22
— © Sheryl L. Nelms	22
A MISTY DAY	22
— © Sheila B. Roark	22
WHERE ARE THEY?	23
— © Sheila B. Roark	23
UNDER THE MOONLIGHT	23
— © Sheila B. Roark	23
SURROUNDED BY DARK CLOUDS	24
— © Sheila B. Roark	24
AT MIDNIGHT	24
— © Sheila B. Roark	24

SNOW STORM IN THE KITCHEN	24
© by Sheila B. Roark	24
I'LL NEVER FORGET HER	26
© by Sheila B. Roark	26
GRANDPA JOHN AND MAMAW MARY'S HOUSE UP GABE ROAD PAST CLENDENIN, WV.	27
© by Juliet R. Lynch	27
WHAT HAS CHANGED IN YOUR LIFE AND WHAT WILL YOU DO WITH IT	28
© by Juliet Rhodes Lynch	28

The Appalachian Trail Tells a Tale

The Appalachian Trail is more than geography that extends through 14 states and 2200 miles of challenging terrain. For poet Gary Drury, his nonfiction account of his rendezvous with Mother Nature, or, as he describes her, a "cruel, relentless mistress," the Appalachian Trail represented an epic journey. Drury is not a camper. Not a hiker. Not a backpacker, boulder scrambler, athlete, or rock climber. In order to embark on the journey that he undertook in 2014, he says, "I elected to step 180 degrees outside my comfort zone." He began the journey as a novice. By the end, he realized that he had undergone a life-changing event.

But he's a poet. So it was perhaps inevitable that he would turn the images into words when the journey ended. He's writing about his experiences, including the episode where he was nearly carried out in a body bag, and found the physical death to be reaffirming. The journey began, Drury admits, under romantic impressions he gleaned from a National Geographic documentary. There were times when he questioned why he was subjecting himself to the physical ordeal. He was too stubborn to give up. But just as powerful as his determination was his dedication to the deceased family members he honored with his quest, and the chari-

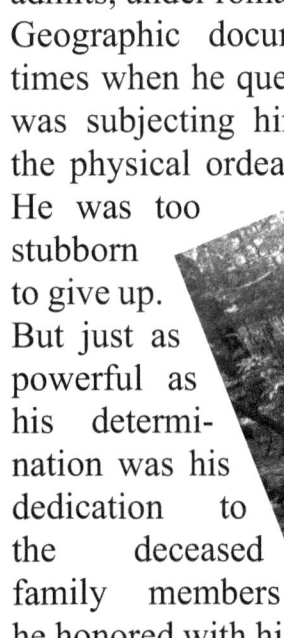

"Risky" Business

Photos Taken by:
Top: A.T. Conservatory personal.
Bottom Left: "Angie", Bottom Right: "Texas"

ties, including the Red Cross, St. Jude's, and the Salvation Army that he supported with his hiking.

He got the idea from fellow hikers who, as they shared their experiences, told Drury that he should put his in print. "My memories, experiences, socialization will last a lifetime." He answered with warm inviting smile and a campfire glow gleaming in his slate-gray eyes. The working title of his book *MY FEET ON FIRE* will surely inspire others to seek adventure of their own, perhaps endeavor a journey of the Appalachian Trail.

Not everyone is going to hike the Appalachian Trail. Not everyone wants to, not everyone is able to. But for those who would like to experience the journey vicariously, walking the Trail in Drury's footsteps as they read his words, the book will be a travel guide. Drury's book *MY FEET ON FIRE* can take you to the Trail, where you'll share the struggles and the triumphs of seven months that Drury, battered in body and exultant in spirit, will always remember.

Drury speculates his book will be available sometimes in 2016/2017. He extends a special thank you to all the hikers that made his trek unique, genuine and wonderful during his most trying moments.

Visit
www.garydrury.com
regularly for updates.

**Photos Taken by:
Top: "Fyr Fly"
Right: "Angie's friend"**

PET HEAVEN

There's a place beyond the rainbow
That God prepared with care
So when our pets must leave us
We'll know that they are there.

It is a special sanctum
Where they can rest and play,
Knowing we will claim them
Again some joyous day.

Our bond will be renewed
Just as it was before;
The undying love of a pet —
You cannot ask for more.

I pray for such a Heaven,
For in my heart I know
Wherever He does take them—
That's where I want to go.
— © **C. David Hay**

SILENT TWILIGHT

I miss the call of the whip-poor-will
That echoed through the wood,
And lament the barren stumps
Where majestic trees once stood.

Hush too, the mystic shadow bird
Who hooted away the night,
Then retreated to his vanished den
Before dawn's glowing tight.

The symphonies of twilight time
Were solace to the soul —
Wise men know to leave untouched
What's best in God's control.

How sad the loss of that we love;
Too late we fail to see —
The treasures of the moment
Someday may cease to be.
— © **C. David Hay**

A GRAIN OF SAND

Who am I that GOD should hear
The prayers I utter through the year?
I am but a grain of sand,
But still a part of what HE,S planned.
HE counts each grain and knows that we
Together, make a mighty sea
Of people, who rever HIS ways
And raise our voices filled with praise,
For who HE is and what HE'S done.
For love so great HE gave HIS son,
That we may all receive the choice
To walk with HIM, and hear HIS voice.
— © **Betty Lou Hebert**

RED SUNSET

Clouds rise like foam, behind the dome
Of mountains in the west.
The sun shoots sprays of golden rays
That pierce the clouds soft breast,
And from inside, a blood-red tide
Of color soon appears
And flushes all the vaporous wall,
As darkness slowly nears.
Then when the light gives way to night,
The western sky still shows,
For many miles, in crimson piles,
Clouds tinted like a rose!
— © **Betty Lou Hebert**

A PRECIOUS DAY

The ancient hills in beauty stand
Above this vast and lonely land,
Against a sky of flawless blue,
A soaring eagle scans the view.
The sign of man, a dusty trail,
Winding through the sage and shale.
No sound of man assaults the air.
Only silence everywhere.
Down from the heights on a wintry day,
The frost god flings his jewels away.
Diamonds, lying on the snow,
In icy splendor, beauty show.
Up from the desert, flushed with light,
A thousand wings flash, silver bright,
As small birds rise in disarray,
To greet another precious day!
— © **Betty Lou Hebert**

TRUE LOVE

One day she was there
the next she was gone;
With no word of goodbye
she left me alone.
The fault was all mine
such sorrow I now bear—
I ignored her impassioned pleas
without thought or care;
She loved me as no other
but the truth I never knew
And thus I broke her heart
and lost a love forever true.
— © **Herbert Jerry Baker**

WHAT IS IT?

What is it that we do the best?
That reminds us of those
Days now past, and
Of the days to come?
We blow up things,
Our fireworks we welcome
A new year and we holler and sing
And in our big show
We celebrate our wars,
Our fire bursting into star glow!
We sing of our capacity for war.
Man's sin is showing.
But God sees our awful ways:
Turning from Him to direct our own course.
But He forgives and directs us still!
Oh Blessed Lord, our Kinsman Redeemer!
Our shout of praise rises to You.
Direct our Peace, and in just wars.
May our praise be louder and more sincere
Than all the bombs we drop in fear!
— © **Ken Gillespie**

SOFT WHISPERS II
By The Bend In
The Mighty Wolf River
— © Ken Gillespie

There was an owl who who lived in the woods,
   In the deep, dark woods by the trail,
   And late at night he came out to sing
      Many songs, my ancestors tell.

And he sang of the woods and the flowers there
   By the trail that crossed the stream
   At Estaunaulla where the river bends
      And the big Oak long ago fell.

And he sang of the gold that was buried there
   Neath the Oak by the curve of the river
   Near the town that was there
      til the yankees came
   And burned it. now' no one can tell

   Where the town stood then by
      the bank of the river
   By the curve where the big Oak fell,
   The owl still sings his lonely song
   In the deep, dark words by the trail.

"Come, here's the gold" and the diggers run
   Digging holes in the flowering dell;
   "No! It's over here, no it's over there"
   And they run and they run pell-mell.

How many have perished? No one can tell,
But the owl keeps count and sings his song,
   "Come to Estaunaulla and find my gold."
But some they say think the devil's there.

   And for gold they just dig into hell!
      But they keep a cornin'
      The devil's song hummin'
   And the owl laughs beside his trail.
      — © Ken Gillespie

DAVE'S READY

the new clothes
are ready
and laid out

the little rag rug
is bought

he has all of the supplies
on the list

crayons
thick pencil #2
A Big Chief
rounded scissors
and glue
all sacked up
to go

it's all there

he's met the teacher
and she's pretty
he's seen his room
they have hamsters
and guppies

it will be fun
he knows

now if I
can just let him

go
— © Sheryl L. Nelms

Flames of Mame is a story of a very wealthy man and women who are married and lived in the mid 1800 hundreds and have had to be apart approximately 12 years due to extreme circumstances beyond their control. She being of an Aristocratic family with status and money and him being very rich in his own right.

Flames of Mame weaves in out of the years of separation and their deep affectionate love for each other, how their story brought about an even deeper change in their life styles they had previously lived and known.

Flames of Mame is in an Era of politics emerging, the War, the times of rebuilding war torn South and North, a time of restoring communities and lives. Becoming totally different from whom you were born as, who you have become, by worldly circumstances and changes of your life styles and gathering the hope of Love, and Reunion in a uncharted territory neither expected to find themselves in.

Juliet R. Lynch NEW BOOK **Flames of Mame**, Drury Publishing, Paperback, Pages, Retail $14.99, **ISBN-10:** 0615899528, **ISBN-13:** 978-0615899527 You will find it available wherever fine books are sold. Check with your local book store or favorite online bookstore.

Palm Sunday is a saga about an Italian American family growing up in Brooklyn. The story follows the adventures of this large warm family as they move from Brooklyn to New Jersey and some as far as Florida. However, no matter how far the family is flung from each other they gather each Palm Sunday and Christmas to celebrate the holiday and more importantly the family. The story centers on five female cousins and how they grow and prosper-their loves, joys and sorrows. The story moves between the present time and the past telling of their parents and grandparents and how the family came to this country. The story concerns the grandparents and parents and their lives and fortunes and the children who in turn grow to have children and even grandchildren of their own. Each Palm Sunday and Christmas the family members reconnect and join together sharing their lives.

Palm Sunday
ISBN-10: 0-9770533-9-3
ISBN-13: 978-0-9770533-9-1
Pages: 64 Trim Size: 6" x 9"

Checkout Paperback & Digital Copies
Smoke Gets In Your Eyes, **The Highway Man**, **The Gypsy Fortuneteller**, **Profusion Of Lilacs**, **Museums**, **Giverny**, **Early Scenes of a Marriage**, **A Society of Two**, **Are They Winning?**

Susan C. Barto (Book Reviewer) is a regular contributor to several anthologies, magazines and gazettes and has authored seven books. Barto's books available online and bookstores.

LOVERS WALK THE BEACH

Pristine sand kissed by the waves
shines with a brilliant light
sent down from a shiny sun
so golden and so bright.

Sea Gulls dance upon the waves
and ride the gentle tides
looking for a bite to eat
enjoying nature's ride.

On this torrid summer day
as gulls fly in the air
two young lovers holding hands
speak of the life they'll share.

So, on this day of sharing love
they walk upon the sand
vowing they will always stay
as they hold each others hand.
— © **Sheila B. Roark**

KEEPER OF THE PAST

I still plant new flowers every spring
And wait for colored promises they bring.
I search to find the first star of the night
And make a wish upon it's twinkling light.
Although I know that nothing stays the same,
Still, I won't let the wind forget your name.
I'll keep alive the lovely songs we sang,
Remembering the way our voices rang.
And I will act in days still left tome,
As keeper of the way things used to be.
— © **Betty Lou Hebert**

Book Reviews by Susan C. Barto

A STRING OF PEARLS by Marion H. Youngquist is a novel about the Greatest Generation that takes the reader from the depression through World War II. The story is told through the eyes and experiences of a young girl named Anna Marie Schultz whom we first meet as an eight year old. We travel along with Anna through these history making years and experience this time with her.

We meet her brave mother who is bringing up Anna with the help of her brother and without Anna's father. We don't learn the story of Anna's birth and the mystery surrounding it until deep into the novel. Anna is blessed with not only her strong mother but her wise and compassionate uncle. Anna takes us through the depression years where she learns thrift and enjoys life without luxuries but full of love and caring.

We follow Anna and her friends and family into World War II from Pearl Harbor Day until the end of the War. We learn about the fates of her friends and how the War touches all those around her. We learn how these years shaped, molded, and created the Greatest Generation. A STRING OF PEARLS has characters the reader will care about and root for from the first page to the last. This novel will evoke the time period before, during, and after the War and bring memories to some and a rich learning experience for those who are too young to remember.

Susan C. Barto (Book Reviewer) is a regular contributor to several magazines and gazettes and has authored seven books. Barto's books available online and bookstores.

COLOR MY SOUL, a book of poetry written by poetic artist Gary Drury, paints the soul with colors of love: Love of God, Love of Nature, Love of man for woman. The poetry is colored with all the shades and hues of love in all its forms. Some of the forms are tortured—one poem refers to Edgar Allen Poe and consequently is dark. However, the book sings about love with joyous abandon.

The books are artistic in its abstract form very like a painting. In the poem MY AMUSEMENT about Poe the artist mourns the lack of color in despair where life is like a masquerade. The poems celebrate God and nature and sometimes, again as in the Poe poem flirt with suicide. As the poet celebrates love in all its forms he, in turn, expresses pain and sorrow caused by love. The poet struggles with ecstasy, guilt, pain, and tender emotions in tandem. Sometimes he seems to feel sinfulness associated with loving while at other times he seems to feel in concert with God and nature.

The poet writes about physical love and spiritual love sometimes as though they could be in conflict. He enjoys sensuous touch and heartfelt adoration. The poet is mesmerized and then awakened out of darkness into the light carrying the reader along on his journey toward love's fulfillment.

COLOR MY SOUL, ISBN: 1-4137-6977-2 Available in Bookstores Now! Get your copy of Color My Soul by Gary Drury, ISBN: 1-4137-6977-2, Size: 6 x 9, Pages: 80. Save $'s when you buy direct. To place your order call: 1.240.529.1031

Available everywhere fine books are SOLD.

CANDLE IN THE WIND is a poetry collection about God and love. The poems celebrate the Lord's goodness and show how he guides our lives. The poems show hope and faith that abound with the belief in our Lord. Some poems tell about our angels, our Guardian angels and all Heaven's angels who come to us with help and point the way to enrich our lives. The poems glorify God and give us the hope of the Resurrection and the Second Coming. The poems talk about how the love of the Lord can color and enrich our lives. Like a Candle in the Wind, the light of our Lord can show us the path to take. One poem is in praise of the beautiful four seasons of the year that color our world. One poem describes a garden and others speak of hope even in the face of the death and mourning of our departed loved ones. He sports ten authored books, Candle in The Wind translated into Russian and now available on Amazon.com. This collection of Gary Drury's newest poems should not be missed. It will enrich your library of poetry.

CANDLE IN THE WIND List Price: $14.99 6" x 9" (15.24 x 22.86 cm) Black & White on White paper,158 pages , ISBN-13: 978-1440475207, ISBN-10: 1440475202

Susan C. Barto (Book Reviewer) a regular contributor to several magazines & gazettes, has authored several books.

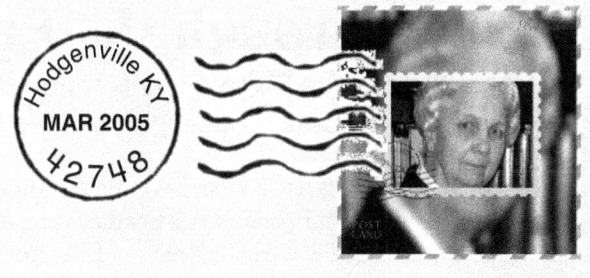

Procula
by Marion H. Youngquist
Celebrating 10th Anniversary 2005 - 2015

Avid readers dive into the Roman era of history and mystery. PROCULA novel sports a wealth of researched historical facts intertwined with mystery and intrigue surrounding Pontius Pilate's wife PROCULA.

Set in Biblical times, Procula. a young girl, is raised by wealthy relatives in Rome. She marries Pontius Pilate, an Army officer, who is sent to Palestine as Emperor Tiberius' personal representative to "keep the peace". When Jesus (a popular Jewish rabbi from Nazareth) is jailed, Procula warns Pilate against involvement. He ignores her. Later, Pilate is summoned to Rome on false charges, but Procula manages their escape. This adventure story, based on historical research, recreates Biblical personalities. Born in a remote village, little is known of this woman until now. The world will never know how her influence could have altered the course of history. See how her own trials and tribulations influenced her life. And later positioned her into a seat of great power as wife to Pontius Pilate. Read for yourself as you take this remarkable journey into ancient Palestine to watch her life unfold. A sophisticated woman of means taunted by powerful imagery in her dreams. When a situation unfolded before Pilate, his wife quickly advised him to be cautious. Had she been more persistent, she may have been able to arrest the crucifixion. Later this caring woman of influence and power seeks sanctuary with her family in AEgyptus, in a small obscure city where they lived under assumed names. Isn't it time you discover the woman who may have changed history?

Enter to Win a FREE Copy of PROCULA

Buy a current issue of The Drury Gazette, include this form page completed with your receipt/invoice, you will be entered into a drawing for a FREE copy of Procula by Marion H. Youngquist (Retail Value $29.99).

Name:_____

Address:_____

_____

City/state/zip Code:_____

Email / Phone #:_____

Mail your entry to: Gary Drury Publisher, The Drury Gazette, 19 West Peachtree Ln, Hodgenville KY 42748.

*Your entry must be postmarked no later than August 31, 2016. Odds of winning are determined by number of entries received. You may photocopy this page, only one entry per The Drury Gazette issue purchase. Winner's allow 6-8 week to receive your prize. Gary Drury Publishing Ministries is not responsible for invalid addresses, lost or stolen mailings. ALL decisions of selected winner are final.

Marion H. Youngquist was born and educated in Salem, Oregon. She was a news reporter in Oregon and Nebraska where she graduated from Midland Lutheran College, Fremont, She also studied at Coe College, Cedar Rapids, IA, UW-Milwaukee, and seminars in Europe. She *scribbles* on planes, ships and in airports--gathering dialog and situations she overhears. For ten years she was a synodical editor and correspondent for The Lutheran and a contributor to other magazines. For ten years she was a synodical editor and correspondent for The Lutheran and a contributor to other magazines. She has written plays for Wauwatosa Village Playhouse. Two full-length plays--The Distlefink and The Gift-Givers--have won prizes as well as her poetry. A poem, Fourth of July Night, was included in a 12-month song cycle by composer Charyl Zehfus. Youngquist also co-authored Little Critters, a children's musical, with Lorraine Brugh, composer, published by Contemporary Drama Service. Procula is her first historical novel, (about the wife of Pontius Pilate) officially released by Drury's Publishing, August 2005. She belongs to the Wisconsin Fellowship of Poets, the Council for Wisconsin Writers, Tuesday A.M. Poets--Milwaukee, and The Dramatists Guild of America. Youngquist and her husband Ted, a retired Lutheran minister, live in Wauwatosa, WI. They have four children, six grandchildren (another deceased), and three great-granddaughters."

Gazing Through the Prism of Life

New collection of effective poems from a thought provoking
award-winning musician-poet

Oceanside, NY – April 06, 2016 – Award-winning musician and poet boons a passionate and discerning pleasure for poetry lovers enthusiastic for life. Musician-Poet Sandra Glassman presents Gazing Through the Prism of Life. Released by Gary Drury Publishing, her literary masterwork touches on themes surely to tantalize readers while inspiring their reading experience

Glassman was considered a child prodigy at age nine. Music was always in Glassman's life and now her music is played on internet radio from South Africa. Sporting two children's book of poetry, published poetry *Chocolate Icing on Vanilla* and Poetic Pastels, two of her poems rest in the Holocaust Museum, Washington D.C. in their archives. *Gazing Through the Prism of Life* displays dedicated and genuine imagination at the poet's deepest core. Embraced with her soulful passion these poems colorfully depict life's happy moments and sorrows in vivid reality. Sandra Glassman's book of fine poetry offers hope, encouragement as it kindles an embodying warmth in the cockles of your heart. She aids readers with encouragement maintain their strength and faith in God.

Sandra Glassman describes her writings as emotional, comical from life's changing times. To her it seems life is changing channels on TV. There is beauty of nature, harsh reality of war, and disbelief of how societies treat their fellow man. Glassman attest plethora awards, medals and honors from various poetry venues. But what brings her greatest joy is sharing her sincerest passion 'Poetry' with others.

About the Author
Sandra Glassman lives in Long Island New York where she is a writer of children's books and a consummate poet. She composes music and has written a classical piece for a book. Glassman is a former piano teacher of twenty years. Most of her wonderful students were young children, and some adults. She enjoys writing poetry where life and fiction cross paths. Music and poetry are a combined force of pleasure for Glassman. She wrote a poem about

our nation's space program that was sent to the White House. Now Glassman's prized framed poem is brilliantly displayed in her family room sporting former President Bill Clinton's signature. Sandra Glassman presently has written over two thousand poems, and recipient of plethora awards. She records music for Emerald Records, located in Nashville Tennessee, Hilltop Records in Hollywood California, and Sun Records in Nashville Tennessee. A year ago, Glassman started guitar lessons which she never thought she would enjoy so much! Sandra Glassman has two lovely adult children Lee and Marrah. Because Glassman was able to read music and play before any structured piano lessons, music has helped her through life's rollercoaster up and downs. Sandra Glassman said "Words are a most powerful weapon, think before speaking."

<u>**Gazing Through the Prism of Life – by Sandra Glassman**</u>
Publication Date: April 06, 2016
Trade Paperback; 14.99; 64 pages; 978-0-692-67026-2

AVAILABLE WHERE FINE BOOKS ARE SOLD.

The Drury Gazette™

Your Advertisement Could Be HERE!?

Mark Stoll's chapbooks and CD's *(Use this order form or a photocopy.)*

Name: _____
Address: _____
City: _____
State: _____
Zip: _____
Phone: _____

ORDER FORM

TITLE	PRICE		QTY	SUB TOTAL
"Rhythm and Rhyme"	@ $6.00 ea.	X	____	$ _____
"More Rhythm More Rhyme"	@ $6.00 ea.	X	____	$ _____
"It's a Coffee House Thing"	@ $6.00 ea.	X	____	$ _____
"Verbal Abuse"	@ $6.00 ea.	X	____	$ _____
"Don't Judge This Book by its Cover"	@ $6.00 ea.	X	____	$ _____
"Stoll Stories"	@ $6.00 ea.	X	____	$ _____
"MS more stuff by Mark Stoll"	@ $6.00 ea.	X	____	$ _____
"Mark Stoll, Acoustic" CD	@ $12.00 ea.	X	____	$ _____

Grand Total Due $ _____

Make check or money order payable and mailed to:

Mark Stoll
P.O.Box 24212
Columbus, Ohio 43224

Postage will be paid by addressee. Please allow four to six weeks for delivery. Do not send cash.

Thank you for your order.

ALL advertisers are solely responsible for their advertisements and products and do not represent the views and opinions of the Drury Gazette or subsidiaries.

TOGETHER AGAIN

The sisters used to be so close
growing and learning each day,
but when they grew up they decided
to live their lives far, far away.

They were too busy to visit their father
the man who chased all of their fears,
the man who loved them with all of his heart
and spent time wiping their tears.

When the Cancer was found by the doctors
attacking him both day and night
his daughters came back to be with him
to help him be strong and to fight.

Once again they were gathered together
supporting their weak and sick dad
talking about the times that they shared
and all of the love that they had.

So, as they watch him get sicker
and fade from their wet, heavy eyes,
they lean on each other to keep going
as they mourn their sweet father's demise.

The girls quietly wait by his bedside
praying that he will not die,
but knowing the time is approaching
when he'll say his final goodbye.
— © **Sheila B. Roark**

A MAN FROM DAKOTA

Within the precinct house there sat
A homeless man with battered hat.
His eyes were gazing at the past.
The sorrow in his features cast
A shaft of sympathy for one
Who felt his life was nearly done.

His name was Bill and he had come
From North Dakota. That's the sum
Of knowledge he supplied and yet,
Somehow we never could forget
The haunted eyes, the hopeless air,
That emanated from him there.

An officer, with camera came
And verified this transient's name.
Then took a picture, capturing,
The essence of Bill's wandering
And when enlarged, it had appeal.
Emotions shown were so real.

It hung awhile up on display
And everyone who passed that way,
Was taken by the quality.
The great despair that all could see.
But now, it hangs upon our wall.
A homeless man, home, after all!
— © **Betty Lou Hebert**

FRESH MEMORIES

I remember days upon the dunes,
Where the ocean sang us salty tunes!
We hiked and sat to stare at all the sand
And hold the warmth of it within a hand.
It sifted through our fingers just like time.
We weren't aware, for being in our prime,
But now in looking back I wonder why
We didn't know that life was passing by!
How different our days then might have been
If for a single moment we had seen
How brief those carefree hours on the shore.
How many years would pass again before
I'd find myself in that same place and see
That being there alone was misery!
Yet I still cling to memories that stay
As fresh as though they took place yesterday!
— © **Betty Lou Hebert**

I SAW MY NAME IN THE SKY

I had a vision in my
mind's eye as I gazed
into that expanse of azure
blue and through imagination
the machination of a dream
came to delight my soul.
I saw my name in the sky
proclaiming that one-day I
would know success
is coming to greet me
and keep me in its palm
to soothe me like a psalm
singing lullaby to calm
my impatient spirit.
I felt its warmth like
a blanket, a full belly
at a lavish banquet
to appease and please
my hungry heart that
threatened to depart
my faith and hope.
Life was a broken remote
that smote my TV screen
blank and black
never coming back
with movie portraying
my dream fulfilled.
My name in the sky
tells me I will not
be a failure 'till I die;
the sky is my blackboard
and destiny signed it!
— © **Gerald Heyder**

SEDGWICK COUNTY
JUVENILE OFFICER
In memory of my father

He always worried about his kids

the runaways who traveled hell
before he found them
the beaten children

the two-year-old he talked about
for days wondered how
a mother could do that
to her own baby

the neglected kids

he cried once for the eight kids
he found living in a miniature house
with seven dogs and rooms full of flies
and dog shit and a bottle of Ketchup

the sexually used kids

men who did that to children
made him mad enough to kill
he said very slowly

in the kids he had hope
always said there was no
such thing as a bad kid

he gave them his best
until he got ulcers and a nervous break down
but his kids always came first
— © Sheryl L. Nelms

LIGHT
Born unto hands of fate
Whether soon or late
Each man must perish
Greet his grim reaper
Implore favorable destination
A noble honorable just soul
Holds kiting glory
A nefarious rogue harden soul
Warriors for peace eternally
Righteousness harbors
Neutral ground
Leveling consequences
Equally and justifiably
Where faith resides
Lovingly in engrossing heart
Each man must harness
Strength despite tribulations,
Overcome inconceivable odds
Light shall pierce darkness
Blazing path to true freedom
Whether soon or late
Each man must perish
Discovering his darkness,
Discovering his Light.
— © Gary Drury

SECRET PLACE

She keeps her private thoughts
in a place only she knows,
found in the deep recesses of her mind
safely hidden from those around her.

Only God is allowed in her secret place
and when she invites Him in
He blesses her with needed peace
and the strength to carry on.

It is here she can speak to God
knowing He will understand
and always ease the pain she feels
as she struggles through her life.

She reserves this place for her sweet Lord
speaking to Him through prayer,
and in return He smiles upon her
gracing her with His deep and lasting love.
— © Sheila B. Roark

ANOTHER YEAR

Another year goes limping by
injured by disaster and war,
heavy from heartache men cannot hide
as they ask what the battles are for?

All people pray as they go through each day
that mankind will finally find peace,
wanting to live in a world full of joy
where sadness and all problems cease.

But the battles keep raging around us
destroying the world that we know
leaving destruction behind them
along with a deeply felt woe.

Maybe next year will be better,
a time when we find blessed peace
and live out our lives with contentment
where sadness and all problems cease.
— © Sheila B. Roark

HERE COMES THE SNOW

The little house stands all alone
surrounded by tall trees
welcoming flakes of falling snow
as they dance upon the breeze.

The icy snow falls gracefully
from gray clouds in the sky,
and covers trees with ermine coats
as hushed as a lullaby.

It also falls upon the house
which shines with crystal light
created by the falling snow
that floats throughout the night.

All is hushed this winter night
now muted by the snow
that gently falls from clouds above
and shines with spirit glow.
— © Sheila B. Roark

THE ELOQUENT EYES

Who is able to translate the passion better,
Than ardent, bright, eloquent eyes,
Who sends you an enigmatic letter,
Who invites you to soar in the sky?
Who tell you something you cannot hear,
Initiate the secret sighs,
Who once now love, now burst into tears?
You, my beloved eloquent eyes!
— © Adolf P. Shvedchikov

MY FANTASIES ARE ENDLESS, YES!

My fantasies are endless, yes!
Don't worry, let my fancy roam,
I have opened doors in my home,
Let them walk wearing a queer dress.
I like the quirks, nevertheless,
Uncover the cage of your mind,
Give me a chance to remind
That mad ideas make progress!
— © Adolf P. Shvedchikov

THE WORLD WILL BE SAVED BY BEAUTY AND ART

In this cruel life where coexists
Heavenly love and dreadful death,
I believe in the beauty's eternal fiesta
To the rest of life, to my last breath!
I don't know how long the terror will rule,
How often new bloody wars will start?
To survive, we must use a reliable tool:
The world will be saved by beauty and art!
— © Adolf P. Shvedchikov

THE WIND DOESN'T BLOW

The wind doesn't blow, all my sails
Have weighed down in the motionless air.
There is long calm, a time of despair,
I think, alas, that all past life fails.
And a vagrant thoughts whisper again
About balance between death and life,
Between sweet peace and bloody strife,
About roses which will wane.
But it doesn't help to suppress my pain,
I cannot transform black into white.
It seems Ecclesiastes was right
To say: everything was in vain!
— © Adolf P. Shvedchikov

KANSAS COMFORT

nothing is
more soothing

than
the barbed

rustle

of fields
full

of tan wheat

waiting
to be

cut
— © Sheryl L. Nelm

IN GRAM'S GARDEN

the back porch is shaded
by white lattice frothed

with pink roses

under the steps
a mossed corner

is full of the delectable sweetness
of lily-of-the-valley

behind the detached garage
stands a long row

of red hollyhocks

along the east side
of the house marches

the royal purple

of iris

and out
in the garden
under the clothesline

blooms three rows of
orange zinnias

covered with
the thick flutter

of yellow butterflies
— © Sheryl L. Nelms

GALVESTON'S EBB AND FLOW

coming
and going

seashells
seaweed

sand smoothed froth

loll of
jelly fish

gull
tracks

turtle
eggs

leaves me
looking

under
rocks
— © Sheryl L. Nelms

BLACK HILLS SPRING

wind rustled

the churn
of meadow grass

hides frogs

strings croaks
out of

every
green stalk
— © Sheryl L. Nelms

BUTTERFLY IN FLIGHT
a monarch
dips

thru the space

between
two

spruce trees

lifts up
and power

dives across
bluegrass

then flip
flip

flips its wings
into an

orange Double Flyer

windsurfing
over

the housetop
— **© Sheryl L. Nelms**

A MISTY DAY
The air is heavy with moisture
creating a soggy blanket
that slowly covers sleeping trees
with an eerie coating of wetness.

Bare limbs can be seen
piercing the heavy fog,
with twisted, arthritic fingers
reaching out from the charcoal mist.

The misty day is tinted gray
and as the fog moves on,
the trees seem to disappear
under a coating of wet grayness.

All is quiet on this day
silenced by the heavy fog
that blankets the sleeping trees
as they dream of the coming spring.
— **© Sheila B. Roark**

WHERE ARE THEY?
It is a hushed and eerie night
as one lone schooner quietly glides
cutting through the lapping waves
of the dancing, dark, and rhythmic tides.

There is no movement on the ship,
no sounds are heard this night,
for her crew has disappeared
though no on knows their plight.

On and on the lone boat sails
with no real place to go,
propelled by the spirit of the sea
it rides the water's flow.

What happened to the crew this night?
We may never know
if they are floating in the sea
awash with spirit glow?

So, on this night the boat glides on
no men or crew in sight,
an empty ship upon the sea
that sails throughout the night.
— © **Sheila B. Roark**

UNDER THE MOONLIGHT
The day has now retired
replaced by the dark of night
lit brightly by a silver, glowing moon
shining down on the serene lake.

The only sounds heard this night
are the steady drone of cicadas,
and the gentle lapping of the water
as it caresses the sides of a lone rowboat.

The couple are enjoying the night
so happy to be together,
enjoying the time they are sharing
lost in a world of their own.

The silver rays shine down on them
lighting them with a diamond beacon
as brilliant as the love they share
on this calm and quiet night.

They stay on the lake for hours,
enjoying the peace of the night
and the completeness they both feel
just sharing each others company.

When it is time to leave
they softly kiss goodbye
and promise to meet again
for they need each other to survive.
— © **Sheila B. Roark**

SURROUNDED BY DARK CLOUDS

Her loneliness attacks her daily
piercing her heart with deep misery
as she numbly goes through her days
under a blanket of dark clouds.

She has no one in her life to love her
no one she can talk to
or share her hopes and dreams,
creating a gaping hole of emptiness
in her being.

Her sadness completely envelopes her
blocking out all happiness and joy,
bringing on unending tears
as she lays in her bed at night alone.

Her fondest wish is to find love
to make her feel whole again,
but for now all she has is misery
and the dark clouds that won't go away.
— © **Sheila B. Roark**

AT MIDNIGHT

The town clock has just chimed midnight,
and by the docks all is quiet
except for the rhythmic sloshing of the water
gently caressing the moored boats.

A blanket of misty fog has moved in
slowly coiling around the boats
swallowing their masts
like a hungry animal after a kill.

The glow from the street lights
eerily shines through the thick fog
creating strange shadows on the deserted streets
on this damp and silent night.

It seems as if all life has been drained
from this part of town
which slumbers peacefully
under a blanket of the foggy mist.
— © **Sheila B. Roark**

SNOW STORM IN THE KITCHEN

© by Sheila B. Roark

Having twins filled my life with pastel rainbows and the golden rays of happiness. Now that they are grown with children of their own, I fondly look back at the time when they were growing up and smile remembering some of their crazy antics. There was never a dull moment during those early years and one day, in particular, comes to mind that I shall never forget, it was the day we had a major snowstorm in the kitchen.

The "storm" occurred on a bright, sunny spring day filled with the joy of rebirth. Trees were budding and animals scampered here and there preparing for the babies that would arrive soon. That day my girls were in a very playful mood. I have to keep a close eye on them, I thought, they look like they're up to no good.

At the age of two and a half, the girls were extremely active and very curious about everything. Exploring was one of their favorite things to do. They loved to open closets to see what they could find. So, when I left them in the kitchen for a few moments alone, they set out on one of their adventures.

After opening two of the closet doors they could reach, Meri found the Tide and Teri found the potato chips and flour. Then the fun began! Meri dumped the entire box of Tide on the floor. Not to be outdone, Teri emptied the bags of potato chips and flour on top of the Tide! Then they preceded to mix everything together, lay on it, and throw it all over the kitchen and each other!

When I returned I couldn't believe my eyes. The kitchen I had just cleaned was coated with a film of snowy white and an occasional potato chip was stuck here and there. The girls were covered in white from head to toe!

It looked like a blizzard had hit the kitchen! They were having such a wonderful time playing snowstorm they didn't hear me when I returned.

There were Tide and flour covering the floor, the counters, the cabinets, the sink, the kitchen table, the kitchen carpet, and of course, all over the girls. They looked like little snowmen with hazel eyes.

I just stood there with my mouth opened not able to say a word. After the shock wore off, I laughed until I cried. I hugged them both and gave them a much-needed bath and put them in their playpen so they couldn't get into any more trouble, at least for a while. It took me a long time to clean up the "storm" and by the time I was finished the girls had fallen asleep.

After a lot of hard work everything looked clean again, that is, except the rug. I couldn't get all the "snow" out of it and years later there were still reminders of the day we had a snow storm in our kitchen on a warm spring day.

Yes, they were always quite a handful usually going in different directions and driving me crazy, but I wouldn't have traded them for the world. We learned a lot from each other during those years of trial and error and today they are two of the best friends I have. Even though they are now adults, they still find ways to fill my heart with rainbows by sharing their precious friendship and love with me.

I'LL NEVER FORGET HER

© by Sheila B. Roark

It has been a long time since I have been in the eighth grade, but after almost a lifetime of living, I still remember my favorite teacher from elementary school. She was a unique character, to say the least, and one I shall never forget.

I attended Notre Dame School for twelve years. It was a private girl's school in midtown Manhattan run by a group of very caring and loving nuns. In those days, they wore a full habit which always demanded respect from all the girls who were part of the Notre Dame family. Their flowing black gowns and heart-shaped headpieces emphasized their deep devotion to their calling. Everyone who attended their school loved them dearly, including me. Since they were our surrogate mothers during the day, we called them Mother. The practice in other Catholic schools was to call the nuns Sister, but not at Notre Dame, our nuns wanted their school to be our home away from home, and to have the nuns become our second mothers.

Notre Dame is a college preparatory school which emphasized learning and has very few extra curriculum activities. I had many good teachers during my twelve years at Notre Dame, which has now become a high school, but my favorite teacher was Mother Genevieve.

She was only five feet tall and about six feet wide, with eyes the color of a new spring morning that always shined with an impish twinkle. Her face was as fair and fine as alabaster, and her smile lit up the room. When she got mad, it never lasted long, and in a short time, she would bounce back to her usual cheery self.

She was more than just a teacher, she was an entertainer who would perform in the strangest ways to emphasize our lessons. I remember one day in an eighth-grade drama class she was teaching us how to do a death scene properly. The next thing I knew, she was laying on the floor with her feet in the air. Of course, the class was stunned not knowing what to do. We just stood there with our mouths opened afraid to move. She laid on the floor for about thirty seconds, arose with the dignity of a queen, and as she smoothed out her habit declared, "Now girls, that's how you do a dying scene."

Then there were the days when we would get her annoyed. When Mother Genevieve got mad at us for not paying attention, she would do strange things with her eyes. She would move them back and forth with such speed, we thought they would take flight. Her soft blue eyes became a blur as she scanned the room searching for trouble makers. Of course, this always stopped any noise immediately and enabled her to continue her lesson of the day.

When she wasn't demonstrating dying scenes, or moving her eyes at Mach speed, she was a wonderful teacher. She was able to make our lessons come alive in a way no other teacher could. When she taught us about the middle ages, we could feel the coldness of the castles where kings lived, and the pain the serfs suffered as they toiled in the fields.

When we studied China, she taught us Chinese writing and let us sample some of the food the people eat. She opened up the Asian world to us and helped us understand what it is like to live there.

She also taught us to love our language and to appreciate it's a beauty by analyzing the works of the masters in her own unique way. She would have us read these works out loud so we could savor their magnificence which made these masterpieces come alive for us. She always made her lessons so vibrant that we looked forward to going to school each day. No one ever wanted to miss anything Mother Genevieve had to say.

She had other wonderful qualities besides being a gifted teacher. She was always available to listen and advise if anyone needed a strong shoulder to lean on. She never turned anyone away who needed her help in any way, and tried to be a friend to all.

This woman, who was loved by all, was a combination of a comic, a teddy bear, and a brilliant teacher. She magically opened up the world to me enabling me to appreciate its wonder and beauty. I recently heard that she passed away and feel a tremendous sense of loss over her passing. I often think of her and of all the precious gifts she gave me so long ago. My hope is that every child who attends school is lucky enough to have a teacher like Mother Genevieve so that they too can think back to their school days with fond memories like me.

GRANDPA JOHN AND MAMAW MARY'S HOUSE UP GABE ROAD PAST CLENDENIN, WV.

© by Juliet R. Lynch

The story goes that Grandpa John and Maw Mary were able to marry after he got in touch with her and asked if she would marry him. She said YES, but they didn't meet until the day they married.

Grandpa Foreman was 6 feet tall and 175 lbs , barrel chested man and very strong for his size and worked from day light to dark six days a week and Sunday was his day of rest. Grandpa, paid $2,500.00 for 800-acre farm and found Deed and it was NO GOOD. Had to pay for it second time.

Their house was made of rough sawed lumber with a tin roof. Inside the kitchen was a wood burning stove with side water chambers. On Saturday night the water chambers were filled with water several times so that the wash tub in the kitchen could be filled for baths. Saturday, the day was time for getting ready for Sunday Church and Sunday dinner and a day of rest on SUNDAY, before the farm work week and chores and school, for the kids on Monday. The Saturday started with the gathering of what was needed, to make the Lye soap and getting drinking water and making and storing pies and cakes for the week to come. The pie safe often held 10 to 15 pies and cakes. Some rested on the window sill in early spring and summer, covered with cheese cloth.

Maw always wore her apron and sometimes a Dust cap. She was about 5 feet 10 inches tall, and she began her work as home -keeper, baby watcher and meal fixer, along with mending and quilt making, and nursing the sick and afflicted. "So much to do and so little time to do it in." Paw seemed to cherish the wee morning hours as he lit the gas lights and built the fire in the stove, so Maw could begin the morning cooking with the aromas of ham and eggs and roasted coffee (chickoree) beans "for strong work coffee as the men called it." Biscuits, fried potatoes, gravy and

fruit was either dehydrated or fresh.

One day, an Oxen dragged a sawed log over Grandpa Foreman, he put a wood splint on it and wrapped it in an old sheet, and went back to work. Grandpa Foreman, ran the Saw Mill , Grist Mill, and General Store.

The Family Tree of Foreman's

Harley Foreman, Nona Foreman, Anna Foreman, Oxeys Forman, Homer Foreman, Earnest Foreman, Genive Foreman.

The rooms of the house all had raised hearth fireplaces, handmade straight back chairs in the room and a chair beside the bed. A wash stand and basin to do cleansing and pitcher with water for rinsing. A WHITE Sewing Machine for in the corner (off limits to Children).

Living room had two full beds for guests and straw ticks and homemade quilts and feather pillows. There were Gas wall lights and two straight back home made chairs and a night stand for family the Family Bible.

Dining room had a rough sawed Oak Boards, two benches on each side of the table and one chair at each end for Pa and Ma. Table was set Country Style with food and after meal the table was covered up with a table cloth. There was no refrigerator!!!! If hungry you got a clean plate and uncover left over food. The Pie safe would have 10 to 12 Berry or Fruit pies. Gas wall lights and candles on table.

WHAT HAS CHANGED IN YOUR LIFE AND WHAT WILL YOU DO WITH IT

© by Juliet Rhodes Lynch

Today is a new day and you can make the best of every moment of it, or you can totally make a mess of it. I can watch in the directness of each day and wonder if we have lost the perspective of all that is precious and good in life. We can see the daily click of the clock, and watch the time fly by, then not realizing just how much time is wasted do to petty little things. You intend to do the laundry, write and pay the bills and get them mailed, run the sweeper, and clean out messy areas of the house that are filled with "stuff," that really needs to go to the trash and out the door. There is a list waiting to go to the grocery store, even one for mall shopping or the badly needed trip to area hardware or the bigger trip to Lowe's or Home Depot. The oft times last two trips will include the other part of past wasted time, when painting rooms in the house, or repairing certain things that you have let go. What about the extra electric plugs needed on the Sun Porch, the slight wiring of a small compact freezer you bought to have extra food, for times of 18 to 20 inches of snow no one seems to expect.

Each day filled with changes not always planned, nor are the changes what we have wanted, or did we continue on the directions which came with the changes or plans. Why can't we seem to move forward and onward to the better directions that would help us to make life a more viable better direction? Spend time of experiencing life, and what good things it can bring.

I project my mind to do certain things and even before I get out of bed in the morning I have ideas, on my mind that I really need to tackle for the day and maybe even for the next few days. I am a writer; a painter, crafter and I also have laundry to do and things to get at the neighborhood Dollar Store. Plenty of cleaning, even household chores that need to be done. They don't always get done. I wish I could wave a magic wand to cause all the mind changing ideas of what I want to be, and to get done, before I take my last breath in life.

One never knows if or when they will take their last breath!!! Does this make it of immediate importance of situations, that one should make changes in their lives? What are the changes that have come into my life and what changes do I want? I have found a faith that has grown stronger in me. I have knowledge of miracles that have happened and prayers that have been answered. I have close friends and family that care about me and even though my health isn't what I want it to be, I see the kindness in people who are helping me to deal with humor, the less than delightful walking and climbing situation of my legs and feet. The church we attend has a ramp for people to use that can't climb steps. On Sunday there is a man at our church that stands at the top of the ramp and waits for me to hand him the handle end of my cane and he helps me walk up the ramp. There is a group of family and church people who stand at the edge of the ramp to make sure I don't slide or need assistance. This goes on both going to church and when it's over. Now here is the humor to this, as I am climbing up the ramp or coming down, with all the assistance. There are cars going rapidly by on Route 4. It slows down and people are looking at me climbing the ramp. In their mind they are saying '' how many people does it take to get the ole lady up that ramp"? Usually the traffic goes fast on that road but during the ramp walk and me, it slows down. Lol

I see the world changing and right now not for the better. I see people who are being drawn away from the Lord and seem to have less happiness in their lives. The families' are drawn apart by addictive lives, such as television, cell phones, computers, drinking, drugs, abuse, divorce, robberies, and killings and soliciting. What else has come to our life, and brings terror to us, shootings, wars, and diseases.

You realize that all these things in our lives do not mean a thing as long as we don't have the Lord Jesus Christ in our lives? Your saying,'' well that's your business and not mine. I am not into religion or going to church." The TRUTH IS, THAT YOU MAY NEVER FIND PEACE AND YOU MAY NEVER KNOW HEAVEN IN YOUR LIFE. "WHO ARE YOU TO SAY THIS? YOU ARE NOT TO JUDGE ME".!!! I'm not judging you but I have come to the realization that in my own life there is a void when there is "STUFF". There needs to be guidance as there was in our parents and grandparents times. That, was what kept us in many areas of our lives. That was the right ways and the wrong ways of doing most everything. In most homes, God and the Bible were in the spirit of how we lived and in the roll of how we acted, and in what we believed in, that was RIGHT AND WHAT WAS WRONG. God ruled, AND was and always should be first in our lives. The father was most generally the head of the houschold. God is

REAL and so is the DEVIL. The President and his ruling parties were backed by God, in their selection of what was to come then, now and in the future. Then, came PRAYERS OUT OF SCHOOL, THE FLAG WAS NOT PLEDGED TO, RULES CHANGED. MASSIVE terror, in Foreign Countries. Governments trying to take over every aspect of our lives. PEOPLE TURNING AGAINST EACH OTHER OVER RELIGION, greed for wanting what will set them free from their own countries, dictators and non-freedom.

We have lost our way and allow ourselves to be prisoners of greed, hate and destruction. We NEED TO CHANGE AND WE CAN IF WE ALLOW GOD BACK INTO OUR LIVES ON A MINUTE TO MINUTE BASIS.

Change is good, but we have to want IT and God, more than we want the sad fakeness of lives filled with all the bad things, that don't matter when you really look at the core of these things that are ''stuff.''

What can we do if we change, how can we make our lives better? We must give the Lord our repentance and ask Him to come into our lives. The commitment of this time making it permanent and giving Him all of ourselves. We must pick up our Bibles and read them and study them. THERE ARE ANSWERS TO EVERYTHING THAT GOD HAS GIVEN TO YOU. GUIDANCE THAT WILL KEEP YOU ON THE RIGHT JOURNEY. The prayers that come down to the very depth of life and just sit down, kneel down and have the daily "little talk with Jesus". That's what makes changes and life changes work. A NEW YEAR and a NEW LIFE, and CHANGES THE HAVE AND WILL MAKE A DIFFERENCE IF YOU CHOOSE AND WILL LET IT.

Submission Edicts
Invite a FRIEND to JOIN the FUN!

1] You must be 18 years or have parent/guardian consent.

2] You must reside in the USA / Canada.

3] You must submit your own original unpublished poem and/or stories.

4] Submissions must be typed on a single sheet of white paper (one side only, no color, no onion skin.)

5] Your complete legal name, address must appear in upper right-hand corner of the page.

6] Only three submissions per envelope, NO entry fee.

7] Winners will be determined by Publisher selection. All awarded prizes are final.

8] Amount of prize is based on number of entries received.

9] Deadline for entry is the 15th of first month issue's per quarter.

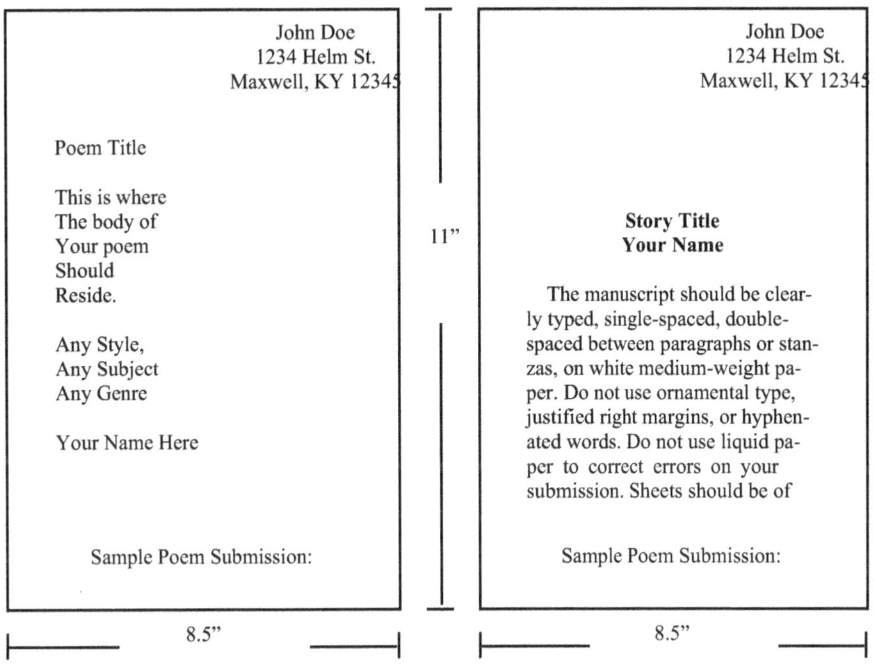

```
                        John Doe
                        1234 Helm St.
                        Maxwell, KY 12345

Poem Title

This is where
The body of
Your poem                             11"
Should
Reside.

Any Style,
Any Subject
Any Genre

Your Name Here


Sample Poem Submission:

|————— 8.5" —————|
```

```
                        John Doe
                        1234 Helm St.
                        Maxwell, KY 12345


        Story Title
        Your Name

    The manuscript should be clearly typed, single-spaced, double-spaced between paragraphs or stanzas, on white medium-weight paper. Do not use ornamental type, justified right margins, or hyphenated words. Do not use liquid paper to correct errors on your submission. Sheets should be of

Sample Poem Submission:

|————— 8.5" —————|
```

GUIDELINES

$0 No reading fees for submission to Anthologies, The Drury Gazette or Theo's Compass. Submission does not guarantee acceptance nor publishing of submitted work. An Author Release Form must accompany ALL Submissions. Submission will ONLY be acknowledged or returned if providing a S.A.S.E. (Self-Addressed-Stamped-Envelope) with proper postage. Always check with the publisher for most current guidelines with a query letter.

Submissions may be Any Subject, Any Style, And Any Genre. Typed. Some restrictions may apply. You are NEVER under ANY obligation to purchase anything at any time. Purchasers are given premium consideration and placement. You may receive offers to purchase publications or services however you are NOT obligated NOR required to buy anything to guarantee publication of accepted work. Whether you purchase or not accepted work is still published.

Accepted submissions will be typed set, a publisher proof mailed to the legal originator for correction of possible errors. Should originator not return publisher proof within the time frame given work will be published "AS IS". ONLY typesetting errors may be corrected at that time. Publisher Proofs are the sole and complete property of the Publisher and MUST be returned.

Submissions are NOT open to the public at large. You must have received a direct mail invitation or been recommended by a past or present author to have your submission considered. If you are submitting an unsolicited manuscript it is required you state the author/publication recommending or sponsoring you. These are Not-For-Profit publications. Supported by my personal funds. Donations or purchases aid in offsetting the associated cost. Submissions NOT adhering to these conditions will be rejected.

The sole purpose of Anthologies, The Drury Gazette, and Theo's Compass is to help authors with limited to no means promote their material. No commercial adverts support or are present in these publications. Included adverts are FREE to book advertisements for authors and FREE or EXCHANGED adverts of publications whose goals are similar.

Anthologies: Every accepted author has their work published for FREE which includes their photo and BIO. The Drury Gazette & Theo's Compass: Every accepted author has his or her work published for FREE, sometimes includes photo and BIO, and the author receives FREE advert space to promote their published book, music, and film or solicited orders. All adverts are the sole and complete responsibility of the advertising party.

* S.A.S.E. = Self-Addressed-Stamped-Envelope
** (Nothing Pornographic)
*** Author may retract submission at any time in writing prior to typesetting or mailed publisher proofs; whichever comes first. No retraction will be accepted if either of these conditions exists without compensation to the publisher for time, expense and delays. Removal requires both author and publisher written agreement.
**** Any use in whole or in part of my copyright material in print or electronically is NOT authorized without my express written consent. Any such use in any published form whether you receive payment or not is strictly prohibited and must monetarily compensate me for such use. You must cease and desist immediately.

IMPORTANT: Author should retain a complete photocopy of the manuscript, not only to facilitate correspondence between editor and author but to serve as insurance against loss of original copy. The Drury Gazette is usually very careful not to lose or damage the manuscript, but my legal responsibility does not extend beyond "reasonable care." Everyone that meets requirements is welcome to submit poems of reasonable length, any style, and any subject matter. There are no fees of any kind to have your poem published if accepted. Any submission may be removed at any time prior to typesetting or mailed galleys. After such time without a substantial valid reason, the author agrees to remit payment to the publisher for the cost of typesetting, galleys, and publishing delays. I reserve the exclusive right to reject any submission without notice for any reason whatsoever. Author release and submission forms available online at
www.druryspublishing.com

Note: Unless specified otherwise - submissions will not be returned. *Poems/Stories should be typed as the example shown above.*

Use of profanity or patently vulgar language — Using language that is racist, hateful, sexual, discriminating or obscene in nature is strictly prohibited and will not be tolerated.

The Drury Gazette™

$0 No reading fees for submission to Anthologies, The Drury Gazette or Theo's Compass. Submission does not guarantee acceptance nor publishing of submitted work. An Author Release Form must accompany ALL Submissions. Submission will ONLY be acknowledged or returned if providing a S.A.S.E. (Self-Addressed-Stamped-Envelope) with proper postage. Submissions may be Any Subject, Any Style, And Any Genre. Typed. Some restrictions may apply. You are NEVER under ANY obligation to purchase anything at any time. Purchasers are given premium consideration and placement. You may receive offers to purchase publications or services however you are NOT obligated NOR required to buy anything to guarantee publication of accepted work. Whether you purchase or not accepted work is still published.

Accepted submissions will be typed set, a publisher proof mailed to the legal originator for correction of possible errors. Should originator not return publisher proof within the time frame given work will be published "AS IS". ONLY typesetting errors may be corrected at that time. Publisher Proofs are the sole and complete property of the Publisher and MUST be returned. Submissions are NOT open to the public at large. You must have received a direct mail invitation or been recommended by a past or present author to have your submission considered. If you are submitting an unsolicited manuscript it is required you state the author/publication recommending or sponsoring you. These are Not-For-Profit publications. Supported by my personal funds. Donations or purchases aid in offsetting the associated cost. Submissions NOT adhering to these conditions will be rejected. The sole purpose of Anthologies, The Drury Gazette, and Theo's Compass is to help authors with limited to no means promote their material. No commercial adverts support or are present in these publications. Included adverts are FREE to book advertisements for authors and FREE or EXCHANGED adverts of publications whose goals are similar.

Anthologies: Every accepted author has their work published for FREE which includes their photo and BIO. The Drury Gazette & Theo's Compass: Every accepted author has his or her work published for FREE, sometimes includes photo and BIO, and the author receives FREE advert space to promote their published book, music, and film or solicited orders. All adverts are the sole and complete responsibility of the advertising party.

Fighting Chance

Fighting Chance is a magazine which features: fantasy, dark fantasy, horror, science fiction, adventure stories, short one-act plays, short-shorts, and poetry.

Love's Chance

Love's Chance is a magazine which features Love and Romance -prose and poetry.

Each magazine will be published annually. There will be a new, expanded format. Single copies are $5.00 per issue. A three-year subscription is $12.00.

Send payment for subscription or individual copies to: Suzerain Enterprises c/o Milton Kerr P. O. Box 60336 Worcester, MA 01606

Guidelines for Authors

Short stories up to 2,000 words - submit one at a time. Poetry not to exceed 20 lines - submit no more than three at any one time. Short-shorts (to 500 words) - submit one at a time.

Submit only camera ready text (no handwriting or page numbers) with author's name following the end of the piece. Use white paper only - any other color will be rejected.

There are no reading fees; there are no payments. Previously published works and simultaneous submissions are okay.

Include SASE with all submissions - otherwise, they will not be returned. The same goes for query letters. No SASE; no response.

Send complete manuscript and/or payment for subscription or individual copies to: Suzerain Enterprises c/o Milton Kerr P. O. Box 60336 Worcester, MA 01606

September Sentiments

EAN13: 9781453653913 Page Count: 104 Binding Type: US Trade Paper Trim Size: 6" x 9" Language: English Color: Black and White Related Categories: Poetry / General. Find it available wherever fine books are sold. Check with your local book store or favorite online bookstore.

www.ingramcontent.com/pod-product-compliance
Lightning Source LLC
La Vergne TN
LVHW061217060426
835507LV00016B/1980